PUFFIN BOOKS

POEMS
for 7-Year-Olds and Under

The rain to the wind said,
'You push and I'll pelt.'
They so smote the garden bed
That the flowers actually knelt,
And lay lodged – though not dead.
I know how the flowers felt.

Specially compiled for children of seven and under, this is an inviting collection of poems, both old and modern, which makes a perfect introduction to the fun of poetry. Among sing-song limericks and boisterous verses from such favourites as Spike Milligan, Lewis Carroll and Roald Dahl are poignant and magical poems from Robert Frost, Walter de la Mare and John Clare.

A classic anthology that will surprise, delight and stimulate young readers, chosen by Helen Nicoll and superbly illustrated by Michael Foreman.

POEMS
for 7-Year-Olds and Under

CHOSEN BY HELEN NICOLL

ILLUSTRATED BY MICHAEL FOREMAN

Puffin Books

Puffin Books, Penguin Books Ltd, Harmondsworth, Middlesex, England
Viking Penguin Inc., 40 West 23rd Street, New York, New York 10010, U.S.A.
Penguin Books Australia Ltd, Ringwood, Victoria, Australia
Penguin Books Canada Ltd, 2801 John Street, Markham, Ontario, Canada L3R 1B4
Penguin Books (N.Z.) Ltd, 182–190 Wairau Road, Auckland 10, New Zealand

This selection first published by Kestrel Books 1983
Published in Puffin Books 1984
Reprinted 1985

Copyright information for individual poems is given on pages 157–60,
which constitute an extension of this copyright page.

Made and printed in Great Britain by
Richard Clay (The Chaucer Press) Ltd,
Bungay, Suffolk

Contents

FAMILY AND FRIENDS

DINNER TIME

SEA AND SHORE

MAGIC AND MYSTERY

JUST VISITING

WIND AND WEATHER

LEAPING AND CREEPING

HI-TECH

FUR
AND
FEATHER

Chicken

Clapping her platter stood plump Bess,
    And all across the green
Came scampering in, on wing and claw,
    Chicken fat and lean: –
Dorking, Spaniard, Cochin China,
    Bantams sleek and small,
Like feathers blown in a great wind,
    They came at Bessie's call.

WALTER DE LA MARE

Yan, Tan, Tether

Yan, tan, tether, mether, pimp.
Sether, hether, hother, dother, dick.
Yan dick, tan dick, tether dick, mether dick,
   bumfit.
Yan bumfit, tan bumfit, tether bumfit, mether
   bumfit, gigot.

ANON.

Cumbrian way of counting sheep: one to twenty.

Flo the White Duck

All white and smooth is Flo
A-swimming;
Her lovely dress is plain . . .
No trimming.
A neat delight,
She fans to left and right
The silver rippled pond.
Behind her, safe and fond,
Her yellow ducklings bob and skim,
Yellow, fluffy, trim.

But all a-waddle and a-spraddle goes Flo
A-walking;
A clacking voice she has
For talking.
In slimy ooze
She plants enormous shoes
And squelches, squat and slow.
Behind her, in a row
Her ducklings dip and paddle
And try to spraddle.

GWEN DUNN

I Saw a Jolly Hunter

I saw a jolly hunter
  With a jolly gun
Walking in the country
  In the jolly sun.

In the jolly meadow
  Sat a jolly hare.
Saw the jolly hunter.
  Took jolly care.

Hunter jolly eager –
  Sight of jolly prey.
Forgot gun pointing
  Wrong jolly way.

Jolly hunter jolly head
  Over heels gone.
Jolly old safety-catch
  Not jolly on.

Bang went the jolly gun.
  Hunter jolly dead.
Jolly hare got clean away,
  Jolly good, I said.

CHARLES CAUSLEY

Poem

As the cat
climbed over
the top of

the jamcloset
first the right
forefoot

carefully
then the hind
stepped down

into the pit of
the empty
flowerpot

WILLIAM CARLOS WILLIAMS

Five Eyes

In Hans' old Mill his three black cats
Watch the bins for the thieving rats.
Whisker and claw, they crouch in the night,
Their five eyes smouldering green and bright:
Squeaks from the flour sacks, squeaks from
  where
The cold wind stirs on the empty stair,
Squeaking and scampering, everywhere.
Then down they pounce, now in, now out,
At whisking tail, and sniffing snout;
While lean old Hans he snores away
Till peep of light at break of day;
Then up he climbs to his creaking mill,
Out come his cats all grey with meal –
Jekkel, and Jessup, and one-eyed Jill.

WALTER DE LA MARE

Haiku

A bitter morning,
sparrows sitting together
without any necks.

TRANSLATED BY
J. W. HACKETT

The Vixen

Among the taller wood with ivy hung,
The old fox plays and dances round her
    young.
She snuffs and barks if any passes by
And swings her tail and turns prepared to fly.
The horseman hurries by, she bolts to see,
And turns agen, from danger never free.
If any stands she runs among the poles
And barks and snaps and drives them in their
    holes.
The shepherd sees them and the boy goes by
And gets a stick and progs the hole to try.
They get all still and lie in safety sure,
And out again when everything's secure,
And start and snap at blackbirds bouncing by
To fight and catch the great white butterfly.

JOHN CLARE

Ducks' Ditty

All along the backwater,
Through the rushes tall,
Ducks are a-dabbling,
Up tails all!

Ducks' tails, drakes' tails,
Yellow feet a-quiver,
Yellow bills all out of sight
Busy in the river!

Slushy green undergrowth
Where the roach swim –
Here we keep our larder
Cool and full and dim.

Every one for what he likes!
We like to be
Heads down, tails up,
Dabbling free!

High in the blue above
Swifts whirl and call –
We are down a-dabbling,
Up tails all!

KENNETH GRAHAME

The Common Cormorant

The common cormorant (or shag)
Lays eggs inside a paper bag,
You follow the idea, no doubt?
It's to keep the lightning out.

But what these unobservant birds
Have never thought of, is that herds
Of wandering bears might come with buns
And steal the bags to hold the crumbs.

CHRISTOPHER ISHERWOOD

Song

I had a dove and the sweet dove died;
   And I have thought it died of grieving.
O, what could it grieve for? Its feet were tied,
   With a silken thread of my own hand's
      weaving.
Sweet little red feet! why did you die –
Why would you leave me, sweet bird! why?
   You lived alone on the forest tree,
Why, pretty thing, could you not live with
      me?
I kiss'd you oft and gave you white peas;
Why not live sweetly, as in the green trees?

JOHN KEATS

The Old Grey Goose

Go and tell Aunt Nancy,
Go and tell Aunt Nancy,
Go and tell Aunt Nancy,
   The old grey goose is dead.

The one that she was saving,
The one that she was saving,
The one that she was saving,
   To make a feather bed.

She died on Friday,
She died on Friday,
She died on Friday,
   Behind the old barn shed.

She left nine goslings,
She left nine goslings,
She left nine goslings,
   To scratch for their own bread.

ANON.

To a Squirrel at Kyle-Na-No

Come play with me;
Why should you run
Through the shaking tree
As though I'd a gun
To strike you dead?
When all I would do
Is to scratch your head
And let you go.

W. B. YEATS

Nipping Pussy's Feet in Fun

(This is not Kind)

Oh Mr Pussy-Cat
My, you are sweet!
How do you get about so much
On those tiny feet?
Nip, nip, miaou, miaou,
Tiny little feet,
Nip, nip pussy-cat
My, you are sweet!

STEVIE SMITH

Cat Asks Mouse Out

(But then Neither is This)

Mrs Mouse
Come out of your house
It is a fine sunny day
And I am waiting to play.

Bring the little ones too
And we can run to and fro.

STEVIE SMITH

Owl

A wise old owl sat in an oak,
The more he heard the less he spoke;
The less he spoke the more he heard.
Why aren't we all like that wise old bird?

ANON.

Christmas

Christmas is coming
    The goose is getting fat,
Please to put a penny
    In the old man's hat.
If you haven't got a penny
    A ha'penny will do,
If you haven't got a ha'penny,
    God bless you.

ANON.

Sing, Said the Mother

Over in the meadows in the nest in
  the tree
Lived an old mother birdy and her
  little birdies three.
Sing, said the mother. We sing,
  said the three.
So they sang and were glad in the nest
  in the tree.

Over in the meadows in the sand in the sun
Lived an old mother toady and her
  little toady one.
Hop, said the mother. We hop, said the one.
So they hopped and were glad in the sand
  in the sun.

Over in the meadows in a sly little den
Lived an old mother spider and her
  little spiders ten.
Spin, said the mother. We spin, said the ten.
So they spun and caught flies in their
  sly little den.

ANON.

The Moo-Cow-Moo

The moo-cow-moo has a tail like rope,
An' it's ravelled down where it grows,
An' it's jest like feelin' a piece of soap
All over the moo-cow's nose.

The moo-cow-moo has lots of fun
Jest swingin' its tail about,
But ef he opens his mouth, I run,
Cause that's where the moo comes out.

EDMUND VANCE COOK

The Fox Rhyme

Aunt was on the garden seat
　　Enjoying a wee nap and
Along came a fox! teeth
　　Closed with a snap and
He's running to the woods with her
　　A-dangle and a-flap and –
Run, uncle, run
　　And see what has happened.

IAN SERRAILLIER

The Old Gumbie Cat

I have a Gumbie Cat in mind,
    her name is Jennyanydots;
Her coat is of the tabby kind,
    with tiger stripes and leopard spots.
All day she sits upon the stair
    or on the steps or on the mat:
She sits and sits and sits and sits –
    and that's what makes a Gumbie Cat!

But when the day's hustle and bustle
    is done,
Then the Gumbie Cat's work is but
    hardly begun.
And when all the family's in bed
    and asleep,
She slips down the stairs to the
    basement to creep.
She is deeply concerned with the
    ways of the mice –
Their behaviour's not good and their
    manners not nice;
So when she has got them lined up
    on the matting,
She teaches them music, crocheting
    and tatting.

I have a Gumbie Cat in mind,
    Her name is Jennyanydots;
Her equal would be hard to find,
    She likes the warm and sunny spots.
All day she sits beside the hearth
    Or in the sun or on my hat:
She sits and sits and sits and sits –
    And that's what makes a Gumbie Cat!

But when the day's hustle and bustle
    is done,
Then the Gumbie Cat's work is but
    hardly begun.
As she finds that the mice will not
    ever keep quiet,
She is sure it is due to irregular diet
And believing that nothing is done
    without trying,
She sets straight to work with her
    baking and frying.
She makes them a mouse-cake of bread
    and dried peas,
And a *beautiful* fry of lean bacon
    and cheese.

I have a Gumbie Cat in mind,
    her name is Jennyanydots;
The curtain cord she likes to wind,
    and tie it into sailor-knots.

She sits upon the window-sill,
    or anything that's smooth and flat:
She sits and sits and sits and sits –
    and that's what makes a Gumbie Cat!

But when the day's hustle and bustle
    is done,
Then the Gumbie Cat's work is but
    hardly begun.
She thinks that the cockroaches
    just need employment
To prevent them from idle and
    wanton destroyment.

So she's formed from that lot
    of disorderly louts,
A troop of well disciplined
    helpful boy-scouts,
With a purpose in life and
    good deed to do –
 And she's even created a
    Beetles' Tattoo.

So for Old Gumbie Cats
    let us now give three cheers –
On whom well-ordered households
    depend, it appears.

T. S. ELIOT

Four stiff-standers
Four dilly-danders
Two lookers
Two crookers
And a wig-wag.

A Cow   ANON.

Three grey geese in a green field grazing
Grey were the geese and green was the
  grazing.

ANON.

Hickety, pickety, my black hen,
She lays eggs for gentlemen;
Gentlemen come every day
To see what my black hen doth lay.
Sometimes nine and sometimes ten,
Hickety, pickety, my black hen.

ANON.

FAMILY AND FRIENDS

Mrs Mason's Basin

Mrs Mason bought a basin,
Mrs Tyson said, 'What a nice 'un,'
'What did it cost?' said Mrs Frost,
'Half a crown,' said Mrs Brown,
'Did it indeed,' said Mrs Reed,
'It did for certain,' said Mrs Burton.
Then Mrs Nix up to her tricks
Threw the basin on the bricks.

ANON.

The Old Gardener

Said the old deaf gardener,
'I'm wore out with stoopin'
   over them impident
   sword-blue lupin.'

'Look at 'em standing
as cool as kings,
   and me sopped to the middle
   with bedding the things.'

HUMBERT WOLFE

from
There'd Be an Orchestra

There'd be an orchestra
  Bingo! Bango!
Playing for us
  To dance the tango,
And people would clap
  When we arose,
At her sweet face
  And my new clothes.

F. SCOTT FITZGERALD

You are Old, Father William

'You are old, Father William,'
    the young man said,
  'And your hair has become
    very white;
And yet you incessantly stand
    on your head –
  Do you think, at your age,
    it is right?'

'In my youth,' Father William
    replied to his son,
  'I feared it might injure
    the brain;
But, now that I'm perfectly sure
    I have none,
  Why, I do it again and again.'

'You are old,' said the youth,
    'as I mentioned before,
  And have grown most uncommonly fat;
Yet you turned a back-somersault
    in at the door –
  Pray, what is the reason of that?'

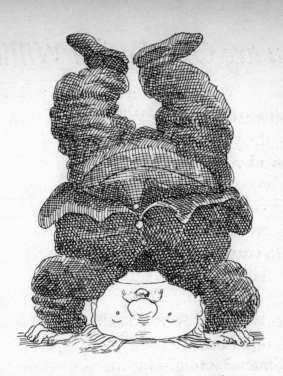

'In my youth,' said the sage, as he
      shook his grey locks,
   'I kept all my limbs very supple
By the use of this ointment –
      one shilling a box –
   Allow me to sell you a couple?'

'You are old,' said the youth,
      'and your jaws are too weak
For anything tougher than suet;
Yet you finished the goose, with the
      bones and the beak –
   Pray, how did you manage to do it?'

'In my youth,' said his father,
  'I took to the law,
 And argued each case with my wife;
And the muscular strength, which it
  gave to my jaw,
 Has lasted the rest of my life.'

'You are old,' said the youth,
  'one would hardly suppose
 That your eye was as steady as ever;
Yet you balanced an eel on the
  end of your nose –
 What made you so awfully clever?'

'I have answered three questions,
  and that is enough,'
 Said his father. 'Don't give
  yourself airs!
Do you think I can listen
  all day to such stuff?
 Be off, or I'll kick you downstairs!'

LEWIS CARROLL

The Legacy

My father died a month ago
    And left me all his riches;
A feather bed, a wooden leg,
    And a pair of leather breeches;
A coffee pot without a spout,
    A cup without a handle,
A tobacco pipe without a lid,
    And half a farthing candle.

ANON.

William I 1066

William the First was the first
   of our kings,
Not counting Ethelreds, Egberts
   and things
And he had himself crowned and anointed
   and blest
In Ten-Sixty-I-Needn't-Tell-You-The-Rest.

But being a Norman, King William the First
By the Saxons he conquered was hated
   and cursed,
And they planned and they plotted
   far into the night,
Which William could tell by the
   candles alight.

Then William decided these rebels to quell
By ringing the Curfew, a sort of a bell,
And if any Saxon was found out of bed
After eight o'clock sharp, it was
   Off With His Head!

So at BONG NUMBER ONE they all
   started to run
Like a warren of rabbits
   upset by a gun;

At BONG NUMBER TWO they were
   all in a stew,
Flinging cap after tunic and
   hose after shoe;

At BONG NUMBER THREE they were
   bare to the knee,
Undoing the doings as quick as
   could be;

At BONG NUMBER FOUR they were
   stripped to the core,
And pulling on nightshirts the
   wrong side before;

At BONG NUMBER FIVE they were
   looking alive,
And bizzing and buzzing like
   bees in a hive;

At BONG NUMBER SIX they gave
  themselves kicks,
Tripping over the rushes to snuff out
  the wicks;

At BONG NUMBER SEVEN from
  Durham to Devon,
They slipped up a prayer to
  Our Father in Heaven;

And at BONG NUMBER EIGHT it was
  fatal to wait,
So with hearts beating all at a
  terrible rate,
In a deuce of a state, I need
  hardly relate,
They jumped BONG into bed like a
  bull at a gate.

ELEANOR FARJEON

Bringing Up Babies

If babies could speak they'd tell
    mother or nurse
That slapping was pointless, and why:
For if you're not crying it prompts you
    to cry,
And if you are – then you cry worse.

ROY FULLER

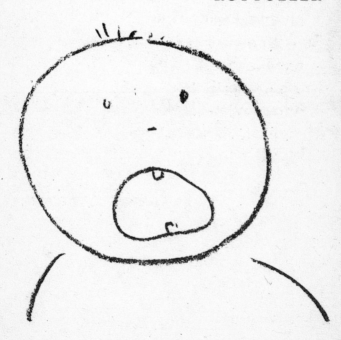

Picnic

Ella, fell a
Maple tree.
Hilda, builda
Fire for me.

Teresa, squeeze a
Lemon, so.
Amanda, hand a
Plate to Flo.

Nora, pour a
Cup of tea.
Fancy, Nancy
What a spree!

HUGH LOFTING

Monday's Child

Monday's child is fair of face,
Tuesday's child is full of grace,
Wednesday's child is full of woe,
Thursday's child has far to go,
Friday's child is loving and giving,
Saturday's child works hard for its living,
But the child that is born on the
   Sabbath day
Is bonny and blithe and good and gay.

ANON.

Father and I in the Woods

'Son,'
My father used to say,
'Don't run.'

'Walk,'
My father used to say,
'Don't talk.'

'Words,'
My father used to say,
'Scare birds.'

So be:
It's sky and brook and bird
And tree.

DAVID McCORD

Dad and the Cat and the Tree

This morning a cat got
Stuck in our tree.
Dad said, 'Right, just
Leave it to me.'

The tree was wobbly,
The tree was tall.
Mum said, 'For goodness'
Sake don't fall!'

'Fall?' scoffed Dad,
'A climber like me?
Child's play, this is!
You wait and see.'

He got out the ladder
From the garden shed.
It slipped. He landed
In the flower bed.

'Never mind', said Dad,
Brushing the dirt
Off his hair and his face
And his trousers and his shirt,

'We'll try Plan B. Stand
Out of the way!'
Mum said, 'Don't fall
Again, O.K.?'

'Fall again?' said Dad.
'Funny joke!'
Then he swung himself up
On a branch. It broke.

Dad landed *wallop*
Back on the deck.
Mum said, 'Stop it,
You'll break your neck!'

'Rubbish!' said Dad.
'Now we'll try Plan C.
Easy as winking
To a climber like me!'

Then he climbed up high
On the garden wall.
Guess what?
He *didn't fall*!

He gave a great leap
And he landed flat
In the crook of the tree-trunk –
Right on the cat!

The cat gave a yell
And sprang to the ground,
Pleased as Punch to be
Safe and sound.

So it's smiling and smirking,
Smug as can be,
But poor old Dad's
Still

Stuck
Up
The
Tree!

KIT WRIGHT

Jack Spratt could eat no fat,
    His wife could eat no lean.
And so between them both, you see,
    They licked the platter clean.

ANON.

There was a young man from Bengal
Who went to a fancy dress ball.
    He went just for fun
    Dressed up as a bun,
And a dog ate him up in the hall.

ANON.

Hey diddle diddle,
The cat and the fiddle,
The cow jumped over the moon;
The little dog laughed
To see such sport,
And the dish ran away with the spoon.

ANON.

DINNER TIME

Grace for a Child

Here a little child I stand,
Heaving up my either hand;
Cold as Paddocks* though they be,
Here I lift them up to Thee,
For a Benizon to fall
On our meat, and on us all.   Amen.

ROBERT HERRICK

* Frogs.

If You Should Meet a Crocodile

If you should meet a crocodile,
    Don't take a stick and poke him;
Ignore the welcome in his smile,
    Be careful not to stroke him.
For as he sleeps upon the Nile,
    He thinner gets and thinner;
But whene'er you meet a crocodile
    He's ready for his dinner.

ANON.

A Thousand Hairy Savages

A thousand hairy savages
Sitting down to lunch
Gobble gobble glup glup
Munch munch munch

SPIKE MILLIGAN

Shrove Tuesday, Ash Wednesday

Shrove Tuesday, Ash Wednesday,
  When Jack went to plough
His mother made pancakes
  She didn't know how.
She tossed them, she turned them,
  She burnt them quite black,
She put in some pepper
  And poisoned poor Jack.

ANON.

Jim

Who Ran Away from His Nurse,
and was Eaten by a Lion

There was a Boy whose name was Jim;
His Friends were very good to him.
They gave him Tea, and Cakes, and Jam,
And slices of delicious Ham,
And Chocolate with pink inside,
And little Tricycles to ride,
And read him stories through and through,
And even took him to the Zoo –
But there it was the dreadful Fate
Befell him, which I now relate.

You know – at least you *ought* to know,
For I have often told you so –
That Children never are allowed
To leave their Nurses in a Crowd;
Now this was Jim's especial Foible,
He ran away when he was able,
And on this inauspicious day
He slipped his hand and ran away!
He hadn't gone a yard when – Bang!
With open Jaws, a Lion sprang,
And hungrily began to eat
The Boy: beginning at his feet.

Now just imagine how it feels
When first your toes and then your heels,
And then by gradual degrees,
Your shins and ankles, calves and knees,
Are slowly eaten, bit by bit.
No wonder Jim detested it!
No wonder that he shouted 'Hi!'
The Honest Keeper heard his cry,
Though very fat he almost ran
To help the little gentleman.
'Ponto!' he ordered as he came
(For Ponto was the Lion's name),
'Ponto!' he cried, with angry frown.
'Let go, Sir! Down, Sir! Put it down!'

The Lion made a sudden Stop,
He let the Dainty Morsel drop,
And slunk reluctant to his Cage,
Snarling with Disappointed Rage.
But when he bent him over Jim,
The Honest Keeper's Eyes were dim.
The Lion having reached his Head,
The Miserable Boy was dead!

When Nurse informed his Parents, they
Were more concerned than I can say:–
His Mother, as She dried her eyes,
Said, 'Well – it gives me no surprise,
He would not do as he was told!'
His Father, who was self-controlled,
Bade all the children round attend
To James' miserable end,
And always keep a-hold of Nurse
For fear of finding something worse.

HILAIRE BELLOC

Celery

Celery, raw,
Develops the jaw,
But celery, stewed,
Is more quietly chewed.

OGDEN NASH

Peas

I always eat peas with honey,
I've done it all my life,
They do taste kind of funny
But it keeps them on the knife.

ANON.

The Flattered Flying-Fish

Said the Shark to the Flying-Fish over
    the phone:
'Will you join me to-night? I am
    dining alone.
Let me order a nice little dinner
    for two!
And come as you are, in your
    shimmering blue.'

Said the Flying-Fish: 'Fancy
    remembering me,
And the dress that I wore at the
    Porpoises' tea!'
'How could I forget?' said the Shark
    in his guile:
'I expect you at eight!' and rang off
    with a smile.

She has powdered her nose,
    she has put on her things;
She is off with one flap of her
    luminous wings.
O little one, lovely, light-hearted
    and vain,
The Moon will not shine on your beauty
    again!

E. V. RIEU

Cows

Half the time they munched the grass,
    and all the time they lay
Down in the water-meadows, the lazy
    month of May,
  A-chewing,
  A-mooing,
To pass the hours away.

'Nice weather,' said the brown cow.
  'Ah,' said the white.
'Grass is very tasty.'
  'Grass is all right.'

Half the time they munched the grass,
    and all the time they lay
Down in the water-meadows, the lazy
    month of May,
  A-chewing,
  A-mooing,
To pass the hours away.

'Rain coming,' said the brown cow.
  'Ah,' said the white.
'Flies is very tiresome.'
  'Flies bite.'

Half the time they munched the grass,
    and all the time they lay
Down in the water-meadows, the lazy
    month of May,
  A-chewing,
  A-mooing,
To pass the hours away.

'Time to go,' said the brown cow.
  'Ah,' said the white.
'Nice chat.' 'Very pleasant.'
  'Night.' 'Night.'

Half the time they munched the grass,
    and all the time they lay
Down in the water-meadows, the lazy
    month of May,
  A-chewing,
  A-mooing,
To pass the hours away.

JAMES REEVES

The Vulture

The vulture eats between his meals
And that's the reason why,
He very, very rarely feels
As well as you or I.

His eye is dull, his head is bald,
His neck is growing thinner.
Oh! what a lesson for us all
To only eat at dinner.

HILAIRE BELLOC

This little pig went to market,
This little pig stayed at home,
This little pig had roast beef,
This little pig had none,
And this little pig cried,
   wee-wee-wee-wee-wee,
I can't find my way home.

ANON.

There was a young lady from Lynn
Who was so excessively thin
That when she assayed
To drink lemonade,
She slipped through the straw
And fell in.

ANON.

Peter Piper picked a peck of pickled pepper,
A peck of pickled pepper Peter Piper picked.
If Peter Piper picked a peck of pickled pepper,
Where's the peck of pickled pepper Peter
  Piper picked?

ANON.

SEA AND SHORE

The Tide in the River

The tide in the river,
The tide in the river,
The tide in the river runs deep,
   I saw a shiver
   Pass over the river
As the tide turned in its sleep.

ELEANOR FARJEON

The Owl and the Pussy-Cat

The Owl and the Pussy-cat went to sea
   In a beautiful pea-green boat,
They took some honey, and plenty of money,
   Wrapped up in a five-pound note.
The Owl looked up to the stars above,
   And sang to a small guitar,
'O lovely Pussy! O Pussy, my love,
   What a beautiful Pussy you are,
     You are,
     You are!
   What a beautiful Pussy you are!'

Pussy said to the Owl, 'You elegant fowl!
   How charmingly sweet you sing!
O let us be married! too long we have tarried:
   But what shall we do for a ring?'
They sailed away, for a year and a day,
   To the land where the Bong-tree grows
And there in a wood a Piggy-wig stood
   With a ring at the end of his nose,
     His nose,
     His nose,
   With a ring at the end of his nose.

'Dear Pig, are you willing to sell for one
        shilling
    Your ring?' Said the Piggy, 'I will.'
So they took it away, and were married next
        day
    By the Turkey who lives on the hill.
They dined on mince, and slices of quince,
    Which they ate with a runcible spoon;
And hand in hand, on the edge of the sand,
    They danced by the light of the moon,
        The moon,
        The moon,
    They danced by the light of the moon.

EDWARD LEAR

maggie and milly and molly and may

maggie and milly and molly and may
went down to the beach (to play one day)

and maggie discovered a shell that sang
so sweetly she couldn't remember
   her troubles, and

milly befriended a stranded star
whose rays five languid fingers were;

and molly was chased by a horrible thing
which raced sideways while blowing
   bubbles: and

may came home with a smooth round stone
so small as a world and as large as alone.

For whatever we lose (like a you or a me)
it's always ourselves we find in the sea.

e. e. cummings

Full Fathom Five

Full fathom five thy father lies,
    Of his bones are coral made;
Those are pearls that were his eyes;
    Nothing of him that doth fade,
But doth suffer a sea-change
Into something rich and strange.
Sea-nymphs hourly ring his knell:
    Ding-dong.
Hark! now I hear them – Ding-dong bell.

WILLIAM SHAKESPEARE
from *The Tempest*

Grim and Gloomy

Oh, grim and gloomy,
So grim and gloomy
Are the caves beneath the sea.
Oh, rare but roomy
And bare and boomy,
Those salt sea caverns be.

Oh, slim and slimy
Or grey and grimy
Are the animals of the sea.
Salt and oozy
And safe and snoozy
The caves where those animals be.

Hark to the shuffling,
Huge and snuffling,
Ravenous, cavernous, great sea-beasts!
But fair and fabulous,
Tintinnabulous,
Gay and fabulous are their feasts.

Ah, but the queen of the sea,
The querulous, perilous sea!
How the curls of her tresses
The pearls on her dresses,
Sway and swirl in the waves,
How cosy and dozy,
How sweet ring a-rosy
Her bower in the deep-sea caves!

Oh, rare but roomy
And bare and boomy
Those caverns under the sea,
And grave and grandiose
Safe and sandiose
The dens of her denizens be.

JAMES REEVES

Little Fish

The tiny fish enjoy themselves
in the sea.
Quick little splinters of life,
their little lives are fun to them
in the sea.

D. H. LAWRENCE

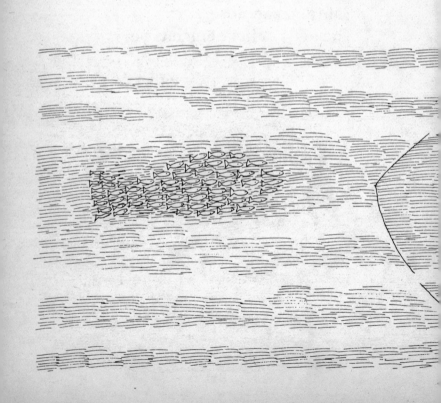

A Baby Sardine

A baby Sardine
Saw her first submarine:
She was scared and watched through
   a peephole.

'Oh, come, come, come,'
Said the Sardine's mum,
'It's only a tin full of people.'

SPIKE MILLIGAN

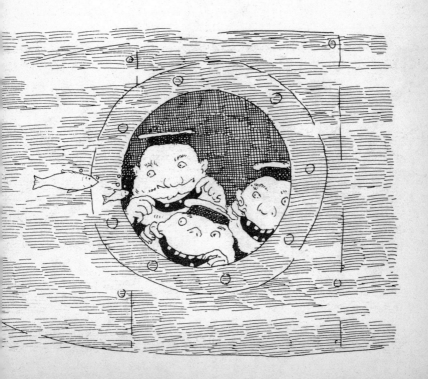

The Octopus

Tell me, O Octopus, I begs,
Is those things arms, or is they legs?
I marvel at thee, Octopus;
If I were thou, I'd call me us.

OGDEN NASH

Round the rugged rocks
The ragged rascal ran.

ANON.

One-eyed Jack, the pirate chief,
Was a terrible, fearsome ocean thief.
He wore a peg
Upon one leg;
He wore a hook –
And a dirty look!
One-eyed Jack, the pirate chief –
A terrible, fearsome ocean thief!

ANON.

She sells sea shells
On the sea shore.

ANON.

MAGIC
AND
MYSTERY

'Twas Midnight

'Twas midnight on the ocean,
Not a streetcar was in sight,
The sun was shining brightly,
For it rained all day that night.
'Twas a summer day in winter
And snow was raining fast
As a barefoot boy with shoes on
Stood sitting on the grass.

ANON.

The Bogus-Boo

The Bogus-boo
Is a creature who
Comes out at night – and why?
He likes the air;
He likes to scare
The nervous passer-by.

Out from the park
At dead of dark
He comes with huffling pad.
If, when alone,
You hear his moan,
'Tis like to drive you mad.

He has two wings,
Pathetic things,
With which he cannot fly.
His tusks look fierce,
Yet could not pierce
The merest butterfly.

He has six ears,
But what he hears
Is very faint and small;
And with the claws
On his eight paws
He cannot scratch at all.

He looks so wise
With his owl-eyes,
His aspect grim and ghoulish;
But truth to tell,
He sees not well
And is distinctly foolish.

This Bogus-boo,
What can he do
But huffle in the dark?
So don't take fright;
He has no bite
And very little bark.

JAMES REEVES

Ariel's Song

Where the bee sucks, there suck I,
In a cowslip's bell I lie;
There I couch when owls do cry.
On the bat's back I do fly
After summer merrily.
Merrily, merrily shall I live now,
Under the blossom that hangs on the bough.

WILLIAM SHAKESPEARE
from *The Tempest*

The Witches' Ride

Over the hills
Where the edge of light
Deepens and darkens
To ebony night,
Narrow hats high
Above yellow bead eyes,
The tatter-haired witches
Ride through the skies.
Over the seas
Where the flat fishes sleep
Wrapped in the slap of the slippery deep,
Over the peaks
Where the black trees are bare,
Where the boney birds quiver
They glide through the air.
Silently humming
A horrible tune,
They sweep through the stillness
To sit on the moon.

KARLA KUSKIN

My Cats

(a witch speaks)

I like to toss him up and down
A heavy cat weighs half a Crown
With a hey do diddle my cat Brown.

I like to pinch him on the sly
When nobody is passing by
With a hey do diddle my cat Fry.

I like to ruffle up his pride
And watch him skip and turn aside
With a hey do diddle my cat Hyde.

Hey Brown and Fry and Hyde my cats
That sit on tombstones for your mats.

STEVIE SMITH

Countdown

There are ten ghosts in the pantry,
There are nine upon the stairs,
There are eight ghosts in the attic,
There are seven on the chairs,
There are six within the kitchen,
There are five along the hall,
There are four upon the ceiling,
There are three upon the wall,
There are two ghosts on the carpet,
Doing things that ghosts will do,
There is one ghost right behind me
Who is oh so quiet . . . BOO.

JACK PRELUTSKY

The Ride-by-Nights

Up on their brooms the Witches stream,
Crooked and black in the crescent's gleam;
One foot high, and one foot low,
Bearded, cloaked, and cowled they go.
'Neath Charlie's Wain they twitter
   and tweet,
And away they swarm 'neath the
   Dragon's feet,
With a whoop and a flutter they
   swing and sway,
And surge pell-mell down the Milky Way.

Between the legs of the glittering Chair
They hover and squeak in the empty air.
Then round they swoop past the
   glimmering Lion
To where Sirius barks behind huge Orion;
Up, then, and over to wheel again
Under the silver, and home again.

WALTER DE LA MARE

Witches and Wizards

From witches and wizards and
   longtail'd buzzards
And creeping things that run
   in hedge bottoms,
Good Lord deliver us.

ANON.

O Moon! when I look on your beautiful face
Careering along through the darkness of
    space,
The thought has quite frequently come to my
    mind
If ever I'll gaze on your lovely behind.

ANON.

In marble halls as white as milk,
Lined with a skin as soft as silk,
Within a fountain crystal clear,
A golden apple doth appear.
No doors there are to this stronghold,
Yet thieves break in and steal the gold.

An Egg

ANON.

JUST
VISITING

Bumble Bee

'Appy 'appy bumble bee
Buzzing amung the tumblin' plums,
Sumetimes, cumin' clumsily
Tha bumps tha tummy on a stump.

DYLAN THOMAS

The Intruder

Two-boots in the forest walks,
Pushing through the bracken stalks.

Vanishing like a puff of smoke,
Nimbletail flies up the oak.

Longears helter-skelter shoots
Into his house among the roots.

At work upon the highest bark,
Tapperbill knocks off to hark.

Painted-wings through sun and shade
Flounces off along the glade.

Not a creature lingers by,
When clumping Two-boots comes to pry.

JAMES REEVES

Grandad

When we go over
to my grandads
he falls asleep.

While he's asleep
he snores.

When he wakes up,
he says,
'Did I snore?
did I snore?
did I snore?'

Everybody says, 'No,
you didn't snore.'

Why do we lie to him?

MICHAEL ROSEN

Sir Smasham Uppe

Good afternoon, Sir Smasham Uppe!
We're having tea: do take a cup!
Sugar and milk? Now let me see –
Two lumps, I think? . . . Good gracious me!
The silly thing slipped off your knee!
Pray don't apologize, old chap:
A very trivial mishap!
So clumsy of you? How absurd!
My dear Sir Smasham, not a word!
Now, do sit down and have another,
And tell us all about your brother –
You know, the one who broke his head.
Is the poor fellow still in bed? –
A chair – allow me, sir! . . . Great Scott!
That *was* a nasty smash! Eh, what?
Oh, not at all: the chair was old –
Queen Anne, or so we have been told.
We've got at least a dozen more:
Just leave the pieces on the floor.
I want you to admire our view:
Come nearer to the window, do;
And look how beautiful . . . Tut, tut!
You didn't see that it was shut?
I hope you are not badly cut!

Not hurt? A fortunate escape!
Amazing! Not a single scrape!
And now, if you have finished tea,
I fancy you might like to see
A little thing or two I've got.
That china plate? Yes, worth a lot:
A beauty too . . . Ah, there it goes!
I trust it didn't hurt your toes?
Your elbow brushed it off the shelf?
Of course: I've done the same myself.
And now, my dear Sir Smasham – Oh,
You surely don't intend to go?
You *must* be off? Well, come again,
So glad you're fond of porcelain!

E. V. RIEU

The Huntsmen

Three jolly gentlemen,
   In coats of red,
Rode their horses
   Up to bed.

Three jolly gentlemen
   Snored till morn,
Their horses champing
   The golden corn.

Three jolly gentlemen,
   At break of day,
Came clitter-clatter down the stairs
   And galloped away.

WALTER DE LA MARE

The Fox's Foray

A Fox jumped up one winter's night,
And begged the moon to give him light,
For he'd many miles to trot that night
Before he reached his den O!
   Den O! Den O!
For he'd many miles to trot that night
Before he reached his den O!

The first place he came to was a
    farmer's yard,
Where the ducks and the geese declared
    it hard
That their nerves should be shaken and
    their rest so marred
By a visit from Mr Fox O!
   Fox O! Fox O!
That their nerves should be shaken and
    their rest so marred
By a visit from Mr Fox O!

He took the grey goose by the neck,
And swung him right across his back;
The grey goose cried out,
    Quack, quack, quack,
With his legs hanging dangling down O!
  Down O! Down O!
The grey goose cried out,
    Quack, quack, quack,
With his legs hanging dangling down O!

Old Mother Slipper Slopper jumped out
    of bed,
And out of the window she popped
    her head:
Oh! John, John, John, the grey goose
    is gone,
And the fox is off to his den O!
  Den O! Den O!
Oh! John, John, John, the grey goose
    is gone,
And the fox is off to his den O!

John ran up to the top of the hill,
And blew his whistle loud and shrill;
Said the fox, That is very pretty music;
    still —

I'd rather be in my den O!
    Den O! Den O!
Said the fox, That is very pretty music;
    still –
I'd rather be in my den O!

The fox went back to his hungry den,
And his dear little foxes, eight, nine, ten;
Quoth they, Good daddy, you must
    go there again,
If you bring such good cheer
    from the farm O!
    Farm O! Farm O!
Quoth they, Good daddy, you must
    go there again,
If you bring such good cheer
    from the farm O!

The fox and his wife, without any strife,
Said they never ate a better goose
    in all their life:
They did very well without fork or knife,
And the little ones picked the bones O!
  Bones O! Bones O!
They did very well without fork or knife,
And the little ones picked the bones O!

ANON.

Sid

Down behind the dustbin
I met a dog called Sid.
He said he didn't know me,
but I'm pretty sure he did.

MICHAEL ROSEN

Three Young Rats

Three young rats with black felt hats,
  Three young ducks with white straw flats,
  Three young dogs with curling tails,
  Three young cats with demi-veils,
    Went to walk with two young pigs
    In satin vests and sorrel wigs;
      But suddenly it chanced to rain,
      And so they all went home again.

ANON.

Busy Day

Pop in
pop out
pop over the road
pop out for a walk
pop in for a talk
pop down to the shop
can't stop
got to pop

got to pop?

pop where?
pop what?

well
I've got to
pop round
pop up
pop in to town
pop out and see
pop in for tea
pop down to the shop
can't stop
got to pop

got to pop?

pop where?
pop what?

well
I've got to
pop in
pop out
pop over the road
pop out for a walk
pop in for a talk . . .

MICHAEL ROSEN

Spring

'My dear,' said Mrs Wren,
   'If Mrs Cuckoo comes to call,
I really think it would be best
   To see her in the hall.
Explaining that our house
   It is so very very small,
We have no room for paying guests,
   Or any guests at all.'

E. LUCIA TURNBULL

from
A Song about Myself

There was a naughty boy
   And a naughty boy was he,
He ran away to Scotland
   The people for to see –
     There he found
     That the ground
     Was as hard,
     That a yard
     Was as long,
     That a song
     Was as merry,
     That a cherry
     Was as red,
     That lead
     Was as weighty,
     That fourscore
     Was as eighty,
     That a door
     Was as wooden
     As in England –
     So he stood in his shoes
     And he wondered,
     He wondered,
   He stood in his
     Shoes and he wondered.

JOHN KEATS

The Lonely Scarecrow

My poor old bones – I've only two –
A broomstick and a broken stave.
My ragged gloves are a disgrace.
My one peg-foot is in the grave.

I wear the labourer's old clothes:
Coat, shirt, and trousers all undone.
I bear my cross upon a hill
In rain and shine, in snow and sun.

I cannot help the way I look.
My funny hat is full of hay.
– O, wild birds, come and nest in me!
Why do you always fly away?

JAMES KIRKUP

Cherry Tree Carol

As Joseph was a-walking
He heard an angel sing:
'This night shall be the birth-time
Of Christ the heavenly king.

He neither shall be bornèd
In Housen nor in hall,
Nor in a place of paradise
But in an ox's stall . . .'

ANON.

Up the wooden hill
   to Bedfordshire.
Down Sheet Lane
   to Blanket Fair.

ANON.

The man in the moon
Came down too soon,
And asked his way to Norwich;
He went by the south
And burnt his mouth
With supping cold plum porridge.

ANON.

There was a young lady from Spain
Who was dreadfully sick on a train,
Not once – but again
   and again and again
   and again and again and again.

ANON.

WIND
AND
WEATHER

Squishy Words

(to be said when wet)

SQUIFF

SQUIDGE

SQUAMOUS

SQUINNY

SQUELCH

SQUASH

SQUEEGEE

SQUIRT

SQUAB

ALASTAIR REID

Storm

They're at it again
the wind and the rain
It all started
when the wind
took the window
by the collar
and shook it
with all its might
Then the rain
butted in
What a din
they'll be at it all night
Serves them right
if they go home in the morning
and the sky won't let them in

ROGER McGOUGH

Windy Nights

Whenever the moon and stars are set,
 Whenever the wind is high,
All night long in the dark and wet,
 A man goes riding by.
Late in the night when the fires are out,
Why does he gallop and gallop about?

Whenever the trees are crying aloud,
 And ships are tossed at sea,
By, on the highway, low and loud,
 By at the gallop goes he.
By at the gallop he goes, and then
By he comes back at the gallop again.

ROBERT LOUIS STEVENSON

Fog

The fog comes
on little cat feet.
It sits looking

over harbour and city
on silent haunches
and then moves on.

CARL SANDBURG

Lodged

The rain to the wind said,
'You push and I'll pelt.'
They so smote the garden bed
That the flowers actually knelt,
And lay lodged – though not dead.
I know how the flowers felt.

ROBERT FROST

The Wind

The wind stood up, and gave a shout;
He whistled on his fingers, and

Kicked the withered leaves about,
And thumped the branches with his hand,

And said he'll kill, and kill, and kill;
And so he will! And so he will!

JAMES STEPHENS

Written in March

*While Resting on the Bridge at the Foot of
Brother's Water*

The cock is crowing,
The stream is flowing,
The small birds twitter,
The lake doth glitter,
The green field sleeps in the sun;
The oldest and youngest
Are at work with the strongest;
The cattle are grazing,
Their heads never raising;
There are forty feeding like one!

Like an army defeated
The snow hath retreated,
And now doth fare ill
On the top of the bare hill;
The ploughboy is whooping – anon – anon:
There's joy in the mountains;
There's life in the fountains;
Small clouds are sailing,
Blue sky prevailing;
The rain is over and gone!

WILLIAM WORDSWORTH

Sir Bunny

Sir Bunny is a splendid shot,
    And every time he fires,
A farmer or a keeper falls,
    Sometimes a brace of squires.

He went out shooting yesterday
    With young Lord Leveret;
But the wind it blew, and the rain it pour'd,
    And both got soaking wet.

ANON.

Windy Nights

Rumbling in the chimneys,
  Rattling at the doors,
Round the roofs and round the roads
  The rude wind roars;
Raging through the darkness,
  Raving through the trees,
Racing off again across
  The great grey seas.

RODNEY BENNETT

The Weather

What's the weather on about?
Why is the rain so down on us?
Why does the sun glare at us so?

Why does the hail dance so prettily?
Why is the snow such an overall?
Why is the wind such a tearaway?

Why is the mud so fond of our feet?
Why is the ice so keen to upset us?
Who does the weather think it is?

GAVIN EWART

Evening Walk

Just as the even-bell rang,
   We set out
To wander the fields
   And the meadows about;
And the first thing we marked
   That was lovely to view
Was the sun hung on nothing,
   Just bidding adieu.

JOHN CLARE

Red sky at night
Shepherds' delight.
Red sky in the morning
Shepherds' warning.

ANON.

A white bird floats down through the air
And never a tree but he lights there.

Snow   ANON.

A house full, a hole full,
And you cannot gather a bowl full.

Fog   ANON.

LEAPING AND CREEPING

from

The Pied Piper of Hamelin

Rats!
They fought the dogs and killed the cats,
  And bit the babies in the cradles,
And ate the cheeses out of the vats,
  And licked the soup from the cooks'
    own ladles,
Split open the kegs of salted sprats,
Made nests inside men's Sunday hats,
And even spoiled the women's chats
  By drowning their speaking
  With shrieking and squeaking
In fifty different sharps and flats.

ROBERT BROWNING

The Frog

What a wonderful bird the frog are:–
When he sit, he stand almost;
When he hop, he fly almost.
He ain't got no sense hardly;
He ain't got no tail hardly either,
When he sit, he sit on what he ain't got –
  almost.

ANON.

The Snail

Snail upon the wall,
Have you got at all
Anything to tell
About your shell?

Only this, my child –
When the wind is wild
Or when the sun is hot,
It's all I've got.

JOHN DRINKWATER

from
The Centipede's Song

'I've eaten many strange and scrumptious
   dishes in my time,
Like jellied gnats and dandyprats and
   earwigs cooked in slime,
And mice with rice – they're really nice
When roasted in their prime.
(But don't forget to sprinkle them with
   just a pinch of grime.)

'I've eaten fresh mudburgers by the greatest
   cooks there are,
And scrambled dregs and stinkbugs' eggs and
   hornets stewed in tar,
And pails of snails and lizards' tails,
And beetles by the jar.
(A beetle is improved by just a
   splash of vinegar.)

'I often eat boiled slobbages.
   They're grand when served beside
Minced doodlebugs and curried slugs.
   And have you ever tried
Mosquitoes' toes and wampfish roes
Most delicately fried?
(The only trouble is they disagree
   with my inside.)

'I'm mad for crispy wasp-stings on a
   piece of buttered toast,
And pickled spines of porcupines.
   And then a gorgeous roast
Of dragon's flesh, well hung, not fresh –
It costs a pound at most,
(And comes to you in barrels if you
   order it by post.)

'I crave the tasty tentacles of octopi
   for tea
I like hot-dogs, I LOVE hot-frogs,
   and surely you'll agree
A plate of soil with engine oil's
A super recipe.
(I hardly need to mention that it's
   practically free.)

'For dinner on my birthday shall I tell you
    what I chose:
Hot noodles made from poodles on a
    slice of garden hose –
And a rather smelly jelly
Made of armadillo's toes.
(The jelly is delicious, but you have to
    hold your nose.)'

ROALD DAHL

Butterfly

Down the air
   He falls sun-lazy
Debonair
   Upon a daisy;

Now he drifts
   To fall between
Snowy rifts
   Of scented bean;

And where petals
   Lift in flight,
There he settles
   Hid from sight.

S. THOMAS ANSELL

The Tickle Rhyme

'Who's that tickling my back?' said the wall.
'Me,' said a small
Caterpillar. 'I'm learning
To crawl.'

IAN SERRAILLIER

Incey Wincey spider
    Climbing up the spout;
Down came the rain
    And washed the spider out:
Out came the sun
    And dried up all the rain;
Incey Wincey spider
    Climbing up again.

ANON.

Ladybird, ladybird, fly away home!
Your house is on fire, your children are gone
All except one, and her name is Anne;
She crept under the frying pan.

ANON.

Little Arabella Miller
Found a woolly caterpillar,
First it crawled upon her mother
Then upon her baby brother.
All said 'Arabella Miller,
Take away that caterpillar!'

ANON.

The Song the Train Sang

Now
When the
Steam hisses;
Now when the
Coupling clashes;
Now
When the
Wind rushes,
Comes the slow but sudden swaying,
Every truck and carriage trying
For a smooth and better rhythm,
For a smooth and singing rhythm.

This . . . is . . . the . . . one . . .
That . . . is . . . the . . . one . . .
This is the one,
That is the one,
This is the one, that is the one,
This is the one, that is the one.

Over the river, past the mill,
Through the tunnel under the hill;
Round the corner, past the wall,
Through the wood where trees grow tall,
Then in sight of the town by the river,
Brake by the crossing where white
    leaves quiver.
Slow as the streets of the town
    slide past
As the windows stare at the jerking
    of the coaches
Coming into the station approaches.

Stop at the front.
Stop at the front.
Stop . . . at the front.
Stop . . . at the . . .
Stop.
    AHHHH!

                                    NEIL ADAMS

Eletelephony

Once there was an elephant,
Who tried to use the telephant –
No! No! I mean an elephone
Who tried to use the telephone –
(Dear me! I am not certain quite
That even now I've got it right.)

Howe'er it was, he got his trunk
Entangled in the telephunk;
The more he tried to get it free,
The louder buzzed the telephee –
(I fear I'd better drop the song
Of elephop and telephong!)

ANON.

Building a Skyscraper

They're building a skyscraper
Near our street.
Its height will be nearly
One thousand feet.

It covers completely
A city block.
They drilled its foundation
Through solid rock.

They made its framework
Of great steel beams
With riveted joints
And welded seams.

A swarm of workmen
Strain and strive,
Like busy bees
In a honeyed hive.

Building a skyscraper
Into the air
While crowds of people
Stand and stare.

Higher and higher
The tall towers rise
Like Jacob's ladder
Into the skies.

JAMES S. TIPPETT

from
The Bed Book

BEDS come in all sizes –
Single or double,
Cot-size or cradle,
King-size or trundle.

Most Beds are Beds
For sleeping or resting,
But the *best* Beds are much
More interesting!

Not just a white little
Tucked-in-tight little
Nighty-night little
Turn-out-the-light little
    Bed –

    Instead
A Bed for Fishing,
A Bed for Cats,
A Bed for a Troupe of
    Acrobats.

The *right* sort of Bed
(If you see what I mean)
Is a Bed that might
Be a Submarine

Nosing through water
Clear and green,
Silver and glittery
As a sardine

Or a Jet-Propelled Bed
For visiting Mars
With mosquito nets
For the shooting stars . . .

SYLVIA PLATH

Steam Shovel

The dinosaurs are not all dead.
I saw one raise its iron head
To watch me walking down the road
Beyond our house today.
Its jaws were dripping with a load
Of earth and grass that it had cropped.
It must have heard me where I stopped,
Snorted white steam my way,
And stretched its long neck out to see,
And chewed, and grinned quite amiably.

CHARLES MALAM

Piggy on the Railway

Piggy on the railway
Picking up stones,
Along came an engine
And broke Piggy's bones.

'Oy,' said Piggy,
'That's not fair.'
'Pooh,' said the engine driver,
'I don't care.'

ANON.

Index of First Lines

Index of Poets

Acknowledgements

The editor and publishers gratefully acknowledge permission to reproduce copyright poems in this book.

'The Song the Train Sang' by Neil Adams from *Travelling Light*, reprinted by permission of the author; 'Butterfly' by Thomas Ansell, reprinted by kind permission of *The Countryman*, Burford, Oxford; 'The Vulture' and 'Jim' by Hilaire Belloc from *Complete Verse*, reprinted by permission of Gerald Duckworth & Co Ltd; 'I saw a jolly hunter' by Charles Causley from *Figgie Hobbin*, reprinted by permission of the author, Macmillan Ltd and David Higham Associates Ltd; 'maggie and milly and molly and may' by e. e. cummings from *Selected Poems* 1960, reprinted by permission of Hart Davis MacGibbon, Granada Publishing Ltd; an extract from 'The Song of the Centipedes' by Roald Dahl, from *James and the Giant Peach*, reprinted by permission of George Allen & Unwin (Publishers) Ltd and A. Watkins Inc; 'Chicken', 'The Huntsmen', 'Five Eyes' and 'The Ride-by-Nights' by Walter de la Mare, reprinted by permission of The Literary Trustees of Walter de la Mare and The Society of Authors as their representative; 'The Snail' by John Drinkwater from *Collected Poems*, reprinted by permission of Sidgwick and Jackson Ltd; 'Flo the White Duck' by Gwen Dunn, reprinted by permission of the author; 'The Old Gumbie Cat' by T. S. Eliot, reprinted by permission of Faber and Faber Ltd from *Old Possum's Book of Practical Cats* by T. S. Eliot; 'The Weather' by Gavin Ewart from *Light Verse for Children*, reprinted by permission of the author; 'William I 1066' by Eleanor Farjeon from *Kings and Queens*, reprinted by permission of J. M. Dent & Sons Ltd; 'The Tide in The River' by Eleanor Farjeon from *Silver-Sand and Snow*, reprinted by permission of Michael Joseph Ltd and David Higham Associates Ltd; extract from 'There'd be an Orchestra' by F. Scott Fitzgerald, reprinted with permission of The Bodley Head from 'Sleeping and Waking' from *The Crack-Up* in *The Bodley Head Scott Fitzgerald Vol III*, and with permission of New Directions; 'Lodged' by Robert Frost from *The Poetry of Robert Frost*, edited by Edward Connery Lathem, reprinted by permission of the Estate of Robert Frost, Jonathan Cape Ltd and Holt, Rinehart and Winston Inc; 'Bringing Up Babies' by Roy Fuller from *Seen Grandpa Lately*, reprinted by permission of the author and Andre Deutsch Ltd; 'Haiku' translated by J. W. Hackett, reprinted by permission of Japan Publications Trading Co Inc; 'The Common Cormorant' by Christopher Isherwood from *The Faber Book of Nonsense Verse*, reprinted by permission of the author and Curtis Brown Ltd; 'The Lonely Scarecrow' by James Kirkup from *Refusal to Conform*, reprinted by permission of the author; 'The Witches' Ride' by Karla Kuskin from *The Rose on My Cake*, reprinted by permission of Harper & Row Publishers Inc; 'Little Fish' by D. H. Lawrence from *The Complete Poems of D. H. Lawrence* (William Heinemann Ltd), reprinted by permission of Laurence Pollinger Ltd and the Estate of Frieda Lawrence Ravagli; 'Picnic' by Hugh Lofting from *Porridge Poetry*, reprinted by permission of Blassingame, McCauley and Wood; 'Father and I in the Woods' by David McCord from *Far and Few*. Copyright 1952 by David McCord. Reprinted by permission of Little, Brown and Company and George Harrap Ltd; 'Storm' by Roger McGough from *After the Merrymaking*, reprinted by permission of the author and Jonathan Cape Ltd; 'Steam Shovel' by Charles Malam from *Upper Pasture*. Copyright 1930, © 1958 by Charles Malam. Reprinted by permission of Holt, Rinehart and Winston, Publishers; 'A Thousand Hairy Savages' from *Silly Verse for Kids* and 'A Baby Sardine' from *A Book of Milliganimals* by Spike Milligan, reprinted by permission of the author; 'Celery' by Ogden Nash, copyright 1941 by The Curtis Publishing Company. First appeared in *The Saturday Evening Post*. 'The Octopus' by Ogden Nash, copyright 1942 by Ogden Nash. First appeared in *The New Yorker*. Reprinted